ISBN: 979-8-218-51747-2
A is for Andy
Copyright 2022 Sol and Luna LLC

For permission requests, write to the publisher at the address below:
Sol and Luna LLC
17 Zunis Ave
Tulsa, OK 74104

Brittany Wardlow and Samantha Ryan
Illustrated by Brittany Wardlow

Printed in the United States

A is for Andy

Written by:
Samantha Ryan

Illustrated by:
Brittany Wardlow

Come along so you can see

how housewives teach the

A is for Andy

B is for
Bravo,
Bravo,
f**king
Bravo!

C is for
Catwalks

D is for DON'T TOUCH THE MORGAN LETTERS.

E is for
"Elegance is
learned,
my friends."

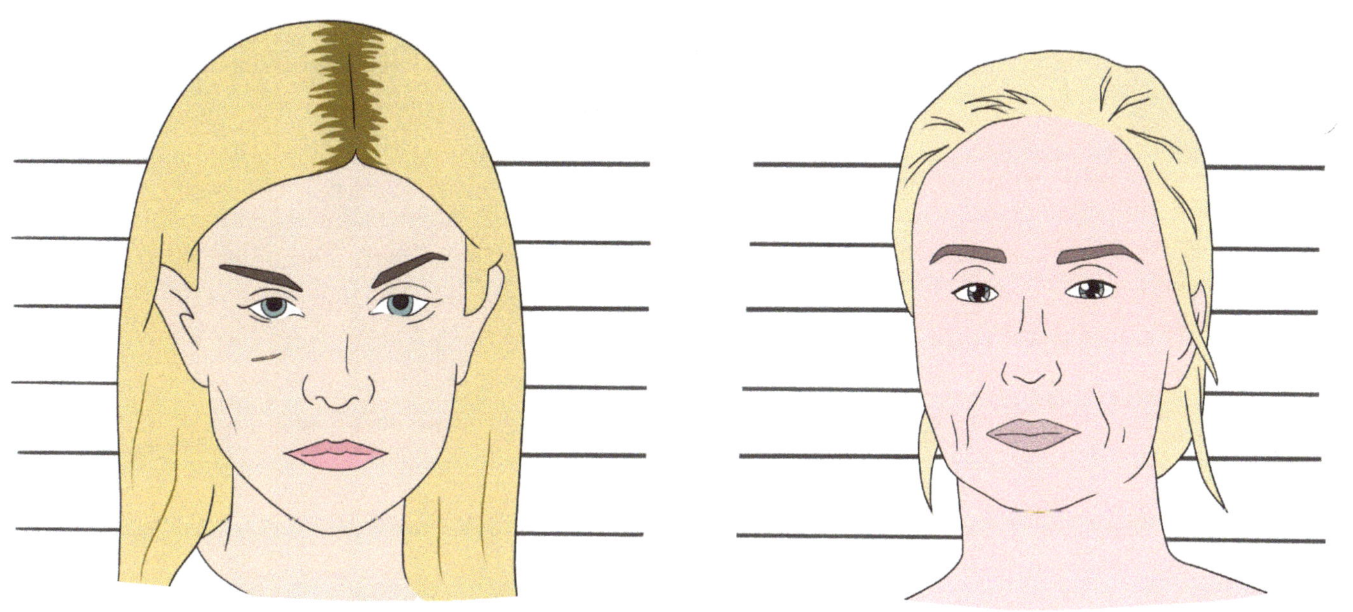

F is for Felonies

G is for
"GOODBYE
Kyle!"

H is for Hunky Dory

I is for "I said what I said."

J is for Jesus Jugs

K is for Kenya! 👏 Moore! 👏 Hair! 👏 Care! 👏

L is for Leg*

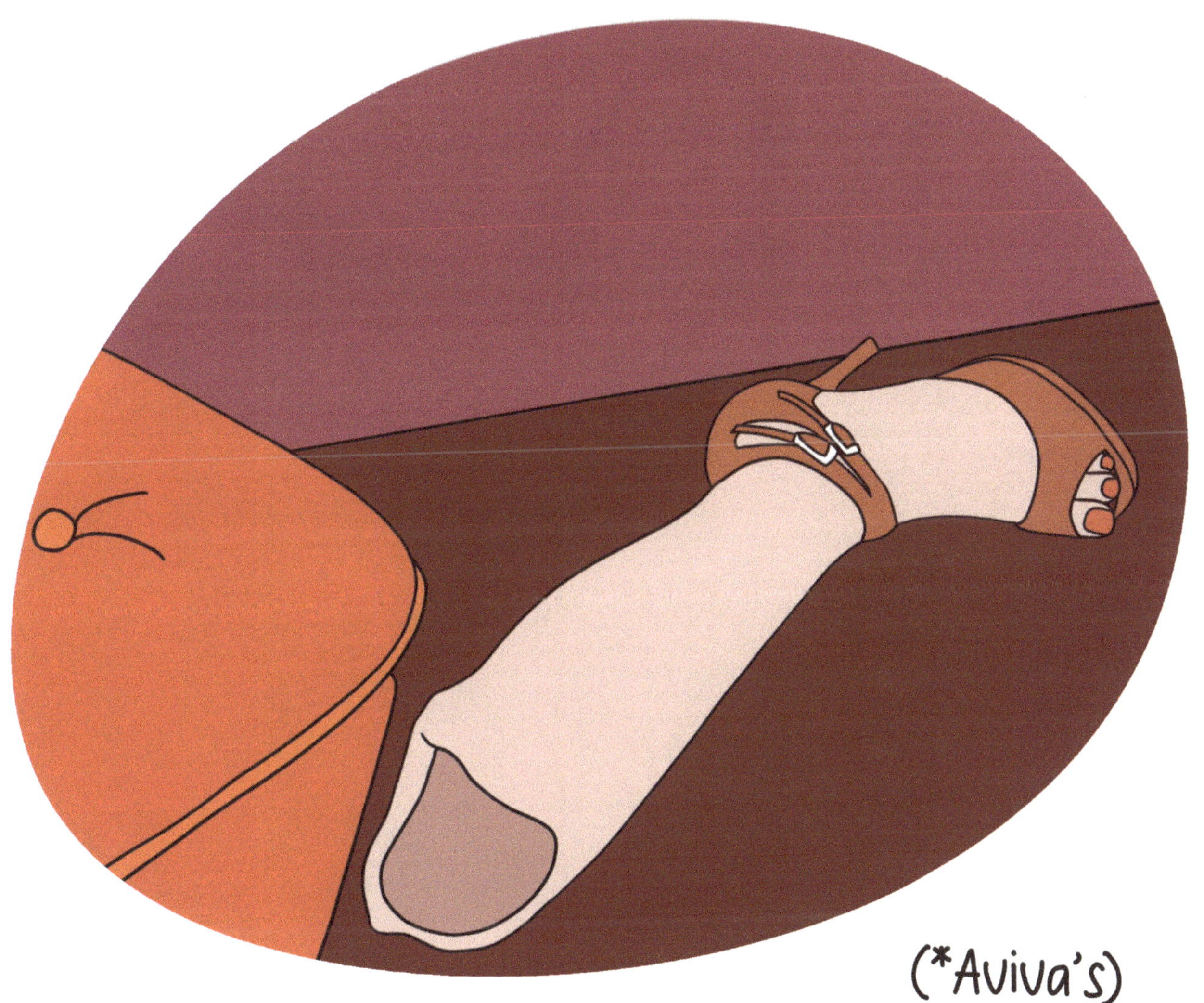

(*Aviva's)

M is for Mention it all!

N
is for Naked Wasted

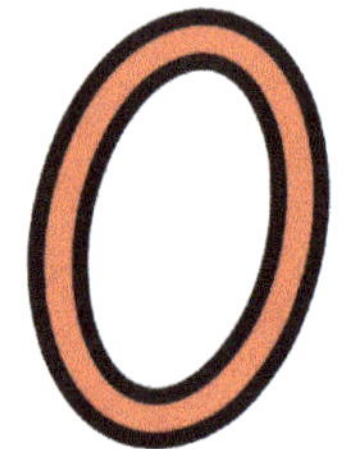 is for the OG of the OC

P is for "Prostitution whore!"

Q is for
of the
Queen
Potomac

R is for Reunions

S is for
Scary Island

T is for Tom's house was broken into and he confronted the burglar and then had to go surgery and then had to go over and then my son, his car five times on the way home, yeah, I'm under a lot of stress. have eye my son and help, he rolled

U is for Uncool

Just be cool, don't be all uncool.

V is for Vow renewals

W

is for "Were people doing coke in your bathroom?"

X is for Xanax. You need to

Y is for "You're a slut pig!"

Z is for Zooming through New York traffic